FREE BONUS TO EASE YOUR ANXIETY

Create your own path to ease your anxiety with Bonnie's exclusive *Cracking the Crazymakers' Code Journal* PDF. Perfect for those readers who want to take action to soar above the chaos. Simply scan the QR code below to download or print your 8.5" x 11" PDF pages and begin the simple steps to your best life!

PRAISE

Bonnie Brindle's *Cracking The Crazymakers Code* is a journey into her personal roller coaster ride of anxiety that can trap people into a life of desperation and despair. Because she understands that many people have experienced similar struggles with anxiety, Bonnie not only shares her story, but gives the reader the process she developed that allows anyone to break the chains of crazymakers. This is a must read for anyone who wants to create the life they deserve!

— **Gary Barnes**
Business and Sales Coach,
Speaker and Best-selling Author
www.garybarnesinternational.com

Cracking the Crazymakers' Code might seem like a short and simple book, but it's packed with ideas, examples, and action steps that will change the way you look at your life and relationships for good.

As Bonnie shares her own experiences with anxiety and examines its causes, I couldn't help but find far too many similarities in my own life. You may not realize how long you've actually been living with and allowing your crazymakers to stay and thrive within you, until you start peeling away the layers as Bonnie has done.

From the simple mantras to visualization techniques to activities in the journal provided, you now have an easy set of tools to take control of the crazymakers within your own life. You have permission to say no to anxiety. Definitely worth the read!

— **Sheral DeVaughn**
Founder of Speaking With Sher,
Communication Strategist/Media Trainer
Author of *The Frog in Your Throat: An Unconventional Primer for Leaping Life's Hurdles*
www.SpeakingWithSher.com

Given all the stress and craziness in the world today, Bonnie Brindle's new book, *Cracking the Crazymakers' Code,* is a must read for anyone longing to find stable ground, and especially for those suffering from crippling anxiety and other stress disorders. Bonnie does us all a favor by sharing the nitty-gritty details of her own anxiety disorder, the crazymaking people and situations that fueled it, and her long and triumphant path to recovery. A seasoned psychotherapist and transformational coach, she provides easy-to-do action steps that can help reset and rebuild traumatized souls and nervous systems. This book is a true gift for those living with high levels of stress and anxiety, and for those who love them.

— **Miriam Zoll**
Author of *Cracked Open: Liberty, Fertility and the Pursuit of High-Tech Babies*
Founding Co-Producer, Ms. Foundation for Women's Original Take Our Daughters To Work Day
Founder of Jin Shin Jyutsu, Northampton
www.jsjnoho.com, www.miriamzoll.net

Can you identify with what it's like to grow up experiencing ever-present anxiety, interspersed with frequent panic episodes? You might feel like hiding out and never moving, never mind ending up writing a book! While our patient/therapist relationship was pivotal in Bonnie's journey, it was not because of some magic on my end as her "shrink". It was because she was ready to begin to address the issues fueling her distress. Recovery from an anxiety disorder isn't an event. It's a life-long journey of evolution. My heartfelt congratulations to Bonnie for having the courage to face her demons with humor and with great honesty. She offers many practical steps for managing anxiety, and she demonstrates that the heart of any recovery is being able to tell the truth!

— **Rich Fitzpatrick, PhD**
www.Fitzpatrick-Psychotherapy.com

Thank you, Bonnie, for sharing your personal story and insightful wisdom! *Cracking the Crazymakers' Code* is packed with emotions, beauty, and pain. By living through multiple childhood traumas and transcending painful, unhealthy relationships, you have shown us the possibility of living a healthy, fulfilling life. Thank you for giving guidance in simple, yet powerful, steps and positive self-talk examples.

— Jackie Schafer, DDS
Co-author of *Expert Advice from Dentists*
Founder of Colorado Healthy Smiles and
Colorado Healthy Sleep
www.coloradohealthysmiles.com,
www.coloradohealthysleep.com

Bonnie Brindle's *Cracking the Crazymakers' Code* is an insightful memoir that provides practical steps for overcoming anxiety. Drawing from her personal journey, Bonnie shares relatable struggles and hard-earned wisdom to guide readers in breaking free from the negative "code" that fuels it. With empathy and encouragement, she offers reflections, mantras, and action steps to help readers reconnect with their strength and find peace.

Bonnie's authentic voice and her use of nature and animal imagery create a unique, engaging approach. This book is a beacon of hope for anyone ready to soar above the chaos that creates anxiety.

— **Ted Prodromou**
America's Leading LinkedIn Coach
Author of *The Ultimate Guide
to LinkedIn for Business*
www.tedprodromou.com

Bonnie takes the reader on a thought-provoking, candid journey through her life experiences, delving into the concept of crazymakers—the troublesome people and events that deeply impact our ways of being, causing us to become trapped in unconscious layers of crazymaking chaos.

She walks the reader through how to recognize their crazymakers and break free, using easy-to-apply, proven tools and techniques, with imagery and energy psychology practices that continue to serve Bonnie on her own journey. The reader is guided through each step in a gentle, loving way to restore balance, tap into guidance, and release energy blocks.

In sharing her personal journey of the struggles and debilitating anxiety that she faced, Bonnie is an inspiration—she is living proof that our own crazymakers can be overcome and we can live life with more freedom and joy.

— Shameema Patel
Founder of SeapetalDigital,
Web design, coaching, and consulting
www.seapetaldigital.com

The familiar feelings of a moment of anxiety, a place of panic, of being fearful and overwhelmed are found throughout the pages of *Cracking the Crazymakers'*

Code, but that's not all. Bonnie Brindle takes readers on her arduous personal journey from being paralyzed in panic and anxiety and unable to leave her house, to overcoming and thriving. As a psychotherapist, she guides readers through reflections and action steps to use in calming these often debilitating and life-altering challenges she calls crazymakers. With her experience and unique modality, this book isn't simply the common refrain. Ready to try something new? Read on!

— **Tina Brandau, SPHR, SHRM-SCP**
Best-Selling Author
Founder, Success Coaching
Solutions Steps to S.U.C.C.E.S.S.™
www.successcoachingsolutions.com

CRACKING THE
CRAZYMAKERS'
CODE

CRACKING THE
CRAZYMAKERS'
CODE

A MEMOIR

BONNIE BRINDLE

Soul of the Wild Press,
Lafayette, Colorado

Cracking the Crazymakers' Code: 9 Simple Steps to Ease Your Anxiety
Bonnie Brindle
Copyright © 2024 by Bonnie Brindle

The author and publisher are not engaged in rendering medical, psychological, or legal advice through this book. If such advice or other types of expert assistance are required, the services of a competent professional should be sought.

Published by Soul of the Wild Press
Lafayette, Colorado

ISBN (paperback): 979-8-9905247-0-5
ISBN (ebook): 979-8-9905247-1-2
ISBN (audio): 979-8-9905247-2-9
Library of Congress Control Number: Data on file

Editing by Melanie Mulhall, Dragonheart,
www.TheDragonheart.com
Book Design by Journey Bound Publishing,
www.journeyboundpublishing.com

First Edition
Printed in the United States of America

To E.B. (Elwyn Brooks) White, author of *Charlotte's Web* the book that defined my childhood love for animals, for inspiring me to write about animals and real life and for making it acceptable to be my shy, anxious child self who wanted, always, to be in nature and with animals.

And to James "Herriot," (James Alfred Wight) who chronicled his life as a veterinary surgeon using the fictional village of Darrowby, England, in *All Creatures Great and Small*. His stories of the animals and people in his practice gave me great insight into the love and respect required to care for others properly and inspired me to remain in close relationship to wildlife, pets, and livestock. Herriot demonstrated the depth of dedication it takes to truly connect with other sentient beings.

CONTENTS

HOW TO USE THIS BOOK

Note: *The scenarios in this book are real events. I changed the names and characteristics of some people to protect their privacy.*

There are two ways of interacting with these pages. One is to read through the chapters as a memoir, because it is the story of my discovery that crazymakers are behind our anxiety, depression, and relationship stress. Crazymakers can include the people who raised us or with whom we're connected in some way, unhealthy belief systems passed down through generations, or traumatic events we've experienced. They are the source of coding that gets into our DNA and programs us to think, believe, and act in ways that sabotage us.

You may also use this book as a stop-and-learn experience. At the close of each chapter, you will find a reflection tailored to boost your awareness of your own response to the crazymakers in your world. Once you've considered what you want to reflect upon, there is a meditation mantra for you to support changing negative thought patterns to positive ones.

Clearly, sitting meditation isn't for everyone. This mantra is designed to be repeated to yourself through a walk or workout, while driving, or during whatever definition of meditation serves you. It is a positive affirmation. When repeated to yourself, your mantra can interrupt the negative coding of put-downs and fears you may carry and allow your mind to open to a more positive perspective. I greatly enjoy walking in nature while repeating a meditation mantra to myself. What a mood lifter!

Finally, there are action steps. Based on your reflections connected to each chapter, the action steps are useful ideas you can act on immediately and develop into your own healing practice. They will help you build positive connections and release negative coding that blocks your energy.

INTRODUCTION

Seen from the outside, my early life appeared pretty comfortable. I was raised in a lovely New England town by the sea. A well-kept house and yard, fresh food, clean clothes, and lots of friends were a given. I had everything I needed in my own home except psychological safety. For some of us at all times, and for all of us at some times, the world is quite wonderful when we're young. But for those of us dealing with crazymakers and coping with debilitating anxiety, the struggle may have started very early.

But what, exactly, are crazymakers? Sometimes crazymakers are the people who raised us or with whom we've lived or worked. They can also be unhealthy belief systems from generations before us that code negativity and fear in us, or they can be traumas we've endured that hold us hostage in our pain. The crazymakers' code is the sum of negativity you've been taught to believe about yourself. This code may have defined and created your sense of self-worth from an early age, but it serves no purpose in your current life or reality. The good news is, that code can be broken, and you can free yourself from the crazymakers that hold you back so you can begin living your very best life.

When I was growing from tween to teen to young adult, I suffered from debilitating anxiety: an ongoing sense of unease and worry that was somewhat generalized, largely social in the company of adults, and included panic attacks in everyday situations that I felt unable to escape without being noticed. Being in a crowd at a concert, sitting in a movie theater or on a train, standing in a line, and getting on a plane are experiences I was once unable to manage. Moving from my early teens to early adult years, I became increasingly tense and avoided many common places and spaces that increased my discomfort.

Trying to keep track of how I needed to prepare for and behave in varying scenarios made my head spin. I always needed to know where the exits and bathrooms were and how to get to them quickly, and I often needed to stay close to someone I knew and trusted. My mind was on overdrive with the attempt to outthink my anxiety before it took over. Thoughts came at me from too many directions at once and spun around, untethered. With each episode of panic, the world in which I felt free to move about became smaller and smaller, until I was homebound, trapped in the abyss of agoraphobia–the fear of leaving one's home to be in public places, among crowds, and, for some, even wide-open areas. Being anxious in all of these different ways made life very difficult for me to navigate, and I knew something had to give.

At the age of nineteen, I began navigating a path to release myself from the burden of my crazymaking anxiety, though it would be another twenty years before I started to feel comfortable in my own skin. My quest for the answers to solve my anxiety puzzle has been an epic journey and an adventure. I have considered many sources of my mental unrest and sought remedies for the pain that unrest causes us and our loved ones. The anxiety related to the crazymakers' code stems from the secrets and lies we are told and tell ourselves, the addictions and the thieves that steal our sense of safety in the human world.

Learning to manage anxiety can be like breaking an addiction. A friend of mine who struggles with complex, trauma-related anxiety explained it this way: "An addiction? You bet. Any time I allow myself feelings of joy, contentment, or pride, my addiction to feeling guilt, unworthiness, and fear comes roaring back to keep me in self-isolation, detached from others." All of these crazymakers rob us of our birthright of peace, bit by bit, until we create fear bubbles that separate us from joyful experiences and healthy, stable relationships.

Why is it that we often attach more meaning to the negative about ourselves than the positive? Why do we beat ourselves up instead of focusing on our strengths, talents, and gifts? Such mental trash has no place in a healing journey, and it takes practice to be kind to yourself. What I have discovered is that my path toward peace of mind needs constant clearing—you know, like that pile of dirty clothes that always seem to be blocking the washing machine.

As deep and dark as the path through crazymaking anxiety, panic, and self-doubt can be, there is always light awaiting us. What I will share with you here are moments and experiences that may be similar to some of your origin story and current struggles. I've included reflections, mantras, and action steps to help you recognize the roots of anxiety and calm your stress. It's a daily practice, not a miracle cure. If you will walk your path along with me, I can show you how I have responded to these challenges and found relief and joy in my mind and heart. Maybe along this path, you'll find something that will work for you too.

I offer my journey here to assure you that you are not alone if you have been burdened with debilitating anxiety and to demonstrate that you, too, can thrive and not just survive. It's about creating a path out of panic attacks and agoraphobia, obsessive-compulsive behaviors, and social anxiety. It's about releasing yourself from the crazymakers' coding and allowing yourself to experience the joy of living life in a responsive, rather than reactive, way.

Most importantly, it's about *your* recovery from anxiety. It's about your growth, your agenda, and your personal path to become the healthiest, happiest *you* that you can become. You deserve to be free of what is blocking your energy and causing you distress. Please join me on a journey of recovery, one in which you may find your authentic self, free of pain and overwhelming anxiety and experiencing a life of appreciation for your abundance. Let's crack the crazymakers' code together, because the message in this story is about how you can begin your journey to comfort, safety, and peace of mind.

Stories were important to me growing up: fictional stories of great adventure, historical happenings, and the secret lives of animals opened themselves for me in the books I read. And they changed me forever. One of those books was among the best-selling American children's novels of all time, E.B. White's *Charlotte's Web*.

In that story, in a modest barnyard, Charlotte A. Cavatica, the simple and brilliant gray spider, befriended a lonely pig named Wilbur, who was slated to be the Zuckerman family's Christmas dinner. When the gossipy old sheep in the next pen explained to Wilbur in grisly detail how he would be killed when he was fat enough, the poor pig had a panic attack. Sobbing and running about, Wilbur was inconsolable until Charlotte promised she would save him. Soon, she began weaving complimentary adjectives into her web that the people believed were miracles designed to describe Wilbur himself. With her calm, practical, and gentle nature, Charlotte helped settle Wilbur's nerves while she made sure he was admired by everyone who visited the Zuckermans' farm. Instead of becoming supper, Wilbur was kept as the prized pig. This story was one of my childhood anchors, and I often called upon my image of Charlotte to help me through my fears and worries. I was inspired by Charlotte's kindness to Wilbur and the satisfaction she felt in her ability to prevent his demise.

As I accompany you on your journey, I aspire to White's description of Charlotte, with which he closed the story. He pointed out that it is rare to find someone who can be a good writer and a good friend. For me, Charlotte was both. And I aspire to be both for you, my friend, to inspire *you* to find *your* way back to peace and self-confidence. Let's walk this path together!

1

ORIGINS

I t's difficult to know where to begin to tell a story about how something unwelcome occupied my life. It's not as if anxiety suddenly moved in like a sketchy, bad-smelling roommate. It's just always been with me. In its appearance as panic attacks, starting when my father's drinking and my parents' fighting reached a peak, anxiety had a stranglehold on my mind and body. Seeking remedies to break it was a driving force for me. Living with anxiety and figuring out ways to regulate and balance myself, despite its continued mutation throughout my life, has been my greatest education.

To say it all began with a singular event would be untrue, but beginning as far back as I can remember, I paid attention to details and had extreme responses to sounds, sights, smells, light, and both human and nonhuman animal emotions. Sometimes, lights were too bright, and sounds were too loud. And other times I would observe the intricacies of plants or pick out the birds in every tree around me—things that others seemed to not notice. My sense of smell was acute, and it wove deep memories of places and events.

Fortunately, I always felt a deep kinship, sense of safety, and gratitude for the natural world and animals, both wild and domestic. Animals became my mentors and trees became my guideposts. In certain periods of my life, nature and animals were what saved me from the beasts of anxiety. Who or what, you might ask, are the beasts of anxiety? They are the secrets, lies, addictions, and thieves that many of us high drive, anxious people were born to or have lived among. They are the crazymakers, the shame creators, and the repressed rot of rage that we have tried to bury all of our lives. For us to heal, they must be outed, and their power must be removed.

At the lowest point of my life, after dropping out of college because I became too anxious to attend classes, I was faced with a decision. I could give up and allow anxiety to consume me and cost me my life or I could reach out for the help I needed. Reaching out from that darkness required me to dig deep, but I didn't want to be away from nature and my human and animal friends, so I reached out instead of giving up on myself. I picked up the phone to make an appointment to see a therapist. It was one of the two best decisions I ever made. And because of it, my other best decision—marrying my kind, smart, loving husband—became possible.

Psychological research has shown the predisposition to anxiety, panic, obsessions, and compulsions is understood to be partly hereditary and partly environmental. My parents were anxious in different ways, with my dad abusing alcohol to cover his social anxiety and what I imagine was his guilt about leaving his first family and creating another one that he largely rejected, and my mother feeding us anxious narratives about some terrible fate that would befall our immediate and extended family. My mother was right. One family member died of AIDS, another became financially dependent on her, and a third committed a felony theft.

My siblings and I grew up in a home that looked sound on the outside but was a sham on the inside. We were well provided with shelter, food, and clothing, but our parents were emotionally unpredictable. They moved from enabling to rejecting, to raging, and back again. It was rather like being surrounded by fun house mirrors, only less fun.

When I hear friends describe warm relationships with their moms and dads, I cannot imagine how that would feel. Despite being hardworking and generous, my mother was neither my solace nor my sounding board. Relating to her was an uncomfortable mix of ups and downs. She would proudly tell her friends of my accomplishments, yet when I was sad or angry, she made cruel, private comments about my inadequacies. As a rule, she gossiped about everyone she knew: family, friends, coworkers, and neighbors. Even the dog. She didn't offer much warmth and comfort to me as I grew from a teen to a young adult. And my father was just the ghost of a man who lived with us and whose alcoholism defined him as an embarrassment. I didn't realize that this wasn't a healthy family life. And while I didn't find a sense of comfort and belonging at home, the survival instinct that lay deep inside me did find it with some of the families of my friends.

When my parents met, they were both married and were already parents. They began an affair that lasted more than a decade and produced three children before they decided to divorce and marry each other. That's when I came along. My siblings born during their affair were given my mother's married name and The Big Secret was hatched. I'll never know whether my mother's first husband was in on this or not, but they produced no more children together, despite remaining married for years.

Sometime before my sibling Riley turned twenty-one, the truth came out to our immediate family. Riley planned to marry a high school sweetheart, and until that time it was believed that our mother's first husband was Riley's father. Before the wedding, our mother told this sibling who Dad really was.

My mom dropped this devastating bombshell because she believed my future in-law shared some of the same characteristics as my alcoholic father. She thought sharing the shocking paternity truth would put brakes on the ceremony and save my sibling from making the same mistake that she had. As you might imagine, her plan backfired. Riley remained aligned with said fiancé, and a deep and long-lasting wedge was driven between mother and child.

It was a couple of decades later that the wider network of our extended family was informed about the Big Secret. Apparently, despite the fact that two of my siblings had the same fair skin and blonde hair as their birth father, many people were fooled into believing my mother's first husband had sired them. How this crazy-making setup affected each of us varied. What was clear, though, was that my siblings' biological father ignored them and treated them like they were someone else's kids. This mistreatment extended even through his will. He bequeathed his meager savings to the children of his first marriage and me. My full siblings were left out, though I shared that money with one of them. By that time, Riley was estranged from the family, and our world traveler brother, the one sibling I had a close relationship with, had already passed away.

The fact that I was "legitimate" and carried our father's last name had made for a dangerous lack of trust among the four of us kids. My mother once shared with me that my father denied paternity of one auburn-haired sibling, making the claim that this child must have been the product of another affair he accused my mother of having. And because he was able to publicly acknowledge that I was his own child, my father did sometimes pay attention to me and my interests, like the winter he built a makeshift skating rink for me in the backyard. In any case, when I refer to the rot of rage that crazymaking people and circumstances can create, these are my top examples.

Fortunately for me, there was a bright light in my every day in Crazytown, though his life was cut short. My brother Tomar. I can only imagine how much his appearance must have worried my parents during their paternity charade. Tomar and I looked like twins. Yellow hair, blue eyes, and goofy grins. How anyone could mistake us for not being full siblings was beyond me, but there we were—with different last names and very different treatment from our father. Though that could have created a crazymaking chasm between us like it did with my other full siblings, my relationship with him was unshakable.

Tomar was always up for a laugh and looking for adventure. Like me, he found solace in nature and loved all sorts of animals and birds. He was my comic relief, my friend, and the kind of brother any little sister would love to have. The nine-year span between us didn't matter to him. His little sister "Boop" was worthy of attention and kindness. During my junior high years, Tomar would sometimes drive me to school, picking up a friend or two of mine on the way. We always headed to class laughing at one of his dumb jokes.

Another family member had a BMW cruiser motorcycle, which Tomar would borrow, and I was forbidden to ride. Getting around that rule, I'd meet him a couple of blocks from home, hop on the back, and we'd cruise along the North Shore of Massachusetts while I enjoyed the ocean views and he eyed the girls on the local beaches we passed.

Just as Charlotte was an antidote to Wilbur's anxiety, Tomar was an antidote to mine. He rose out of the chaos of the crazymakers' cauldron, forging his own path. Though he, too, was affected by our family dysfunction, Tomar seemed always to dance above the fray. He had an otherworldly quality about him that reminded me of a butterfly, seemingly avoiding being coated by the code.

When Tomar left home by himself to travel through Europe, India, and Central and South America, I was deeply devastated and certain I'd never see him again. I cried for days. In recognition of my pain, my father surprised me by bringing home a dog to cheer me up.

All yellow-furred enthusiasm and tail wags, he became the horse I didn't have, running around the backyard and jumping over obstacles I set up for him. I named this new family member after my brother. Odd, yes, but that was the size of the hole in 12-year-old me Tomar's absence created.

To my utter relief, Tomar did return safely from his world travels. And some years later, he moved to California. While his new wife was setting up their home in Santa Cruz, Tomar and I embarked on a cross-country road trip to deliver his van. That trip was a joyful highlight of my life, filled with history and nature, an unforgettable adventure with my brother.

Upon returning to the East Coast, I felt Tomar's absence deeply. By this time, I had lost all sense of comfort and safety around my family. Fortunately, I did visit Tomar in California several times, and took plenty of silly photos to prove it. Feeling at home on the West Coast, he'd strike up a friendly conversation with anyone in his orbit. And in his world travels, Tomar had stayed with various families, always working to help them in some way. That he suffered his end from AIDS was a cruel, crazymaking twist for a man whose light had shone so brightly and who had made so many people feel they had met a friend.

The family of origin crazymakers' code lives deep within our core. It dwells in our DNA and in our blood. It is the belief system passed down from generation to generation that becomes the very foundation of our worldview and self-worth from childhood into adulthood.

With encouragement and support from an emotionally healthy family, many people are able to approach life with confidence and self-respect. But those of us who have grown up with constant criticism and shifting moral values are left on shaky ground as we transform ourselves from children into adults. Without a solid foundation of fairness and support when life's challenges arise, we lack the ability to move through life in a confident and balanced way. Instead, we may develop fears and distrust of others and become untrustworthy ourselves. All of this anxiety is a recipe for relationship struggles and disappointment.

Both my parents were liars and cheats in their relationships, so it follows that the next generation might struggle with honesty and intimacy. My mom had serial affairs with a number of married men, some of whose wives she counted as friends. She may have inherited this behavior of betrayal from her father, who impregnated a woman at the same time he was preparing to marry my grandmother. That pattern of deceit flowed into my own generation.

When my mom's relationship with a man whose family spent many Sunday afternoons with us was discovered, their highly anxious daughter, who was among my most valued friends, shut down completely. And she shut me out for good. That crazymaking loss was overwhelming for me, and further distanced me from my mom.

Generational crazymakers' coding sticks and is passed on. For a time as a young woman, I was a magnet for attracting narcissistic, unfaithful men as partners.

Because I reached out for help in my early twenties, I was able to change my coding and begin to attract safer relationships. But it certainly didn't happen overnight.

Maybe some of this sounds familiar to you. This crazymaking generational inheritance is more common than most of us realize or are able to admit. And it can certainly be part of why you may be struggling to find healthy and secure friendships and love relationships, as well as balanced and respectful relationships with work peers and superiors. And possibly even with your children. Crazymakers' coding is deep and dark, and light is its enemy. Bringing it forth to be acknowledged, revealed, and released are the necessary steps to free yourself from its crazymaking clutches.

REFLECTION

In your early life, what did you think of as normal behaviors or relationships that weren't? Whose actions have you made excuses for or chosen to ignore? What comparisons have you made between your family and other people's families? Have you sought comfort and support in others outside of your immediate family? Why?

YOUR MEDITATION MANTRA

Even if my family didn't always support me, I accept myself, and I am worthy of love.

ACTION STEPS

Take time to sift through your memories and be as honest as possible with yourself. What did you accept in the past that is now unacceptable? In your *Cracking the Crazymakers' Code Journal*, make a list of family beliefs, activities, or behaviors that once seemed acceptable but now do not. Write a few lines about each example and describe your reactions to them, focusing on how you felt then and how you feel now.

Download your free *Cracking the Crazymakers' Code Journal* PDF here:

I always wanted to be outside. 1964

2

CONVERSATIONS

For many years, I've been a psychotherapist in private practice and an educator and instructional coach in public middle schools. The middle years are a tumultuous time. Hormones flood our systems, awareness of the world outside us grows exponentially, and we begin to see adults as flawed individuals.

I was no exception to these experiences, and a significant one involved seeing a major flaw in my father with clarity. I became aware that my father was an alcoholic when I was twelve. I was certainly aware that he drank a lot and that his friends who visited our house often brought whiskey disguised in soft drink bottles. But the lightning bolt illuminating my father's full-blown alcoholism struck me hard. Home one evening by myself before either of my parents returned for dinner, I heard the squeal of brakes and the crunch of metal on metal. As he turned into our driveway, my father broadsided another vehicle, coincidentally driven by one of my siblings' friends.

Dad stormed into the house, hollering about the "goddamned kid's driving" and yanked the refrigerator door open. Tipping up a gallon of milk in one hand, he poured some into his mouth and more on the floor. Watching with a mix of fright and intrigue, I suddenly understood just how bad my dad's drinking problem was. He had caused an accident right in front of our house.

I recorded this incident in my mind as if it were a movie, and when the police came and sat my father down at the kitchen table, I expected them to arrest him or at least detain him to sleep it off, which would have been a relief. They didn't. After telling him to stay home and calm down, they left.

My siblings' friend appeared to be fine after the accident, but I was definitely not fine. I burrowed deeper into myself at home, knowing there was no one I could trust: not my mother, not my father, and not even the police.

This event marked the beginning of my crazymaking nightly vigilance about my father's condition. When he came home drunk and passed out early, I could go to sleep. When he came home later and started fighting with my mother, I often lay awake for hours to be sure things didn't get too out of control. When they *did* get out of control, I didn't call the police. Instead, I tried to separate my parents, with varying results. Sometimes when I would go downstairs and yell at them to stop, they would. But I was not always successful.

The layers of anxiety grew in me, and I began to spend as much time as possible away from our house. Fortunately for me, Carol, a family friend who was aware of my childhood obsession with horses and an equestrian herself, was kind enough to take me on my very first trail ride. My world tilted on its axis. I was immediately and forever changed, and horses quickly became my lifeline. In their presence I could relax, feel joy and connection, and ground myself in their earthly simplicity. And very soon, I found myself with an after-school and weekend job at the local stable.

Horses appeared to be good listeners. Many times, when I struggled to keep my balance and needed a friendly ear, I chose a hairy one. Tomar, and now horses, were two things in my crazymaking adolescent life that helped keep me sane. After feeding and grooming the horses in my care, I often parked myself in the corner of one of their stalls and just watched and listened as they calmly chomped on hay. The combination of the sweet smell of the grasses being munched, the fresh aroma of pine shavings, and the horses' earthy scents was intoxicating. Their energy was incredibly peaceful, and it was the horses who first heard my tales of woe, fears, and failures. They listened without judgment, providing me with a safe space to practice revealing my anxieties before telling them to trusted humans. And because I could tune in to their calm vibrations, I heard their advice for me and felt their support. I always felt so much better after speaking my truth to the horses and listening to their sage guidance.

But no pets or livestock are required for guidance from animals. Any sliver of nature will do. A trail, a park, a backyard, or even a vivid imagination is all you need. Envision animals or notice those around—a squirrel, an insect, or your neighborhood birds—and tune in to them. When you do, they will offer messages of guidance. Indigenous cultures worldwide have set examples to follow. They maintain their deep connections to nature and animals and hold these vital relationships as sacred while many modern cultures have all but abandoned them, to our detriment.

When we reach back to our roots as human beings and reconnect with the energies of the other beings around us, we receive rich guidance to show us our power, strength, and grace. Feelings of loneliness and alienation melt away as we reconnect to the natural world. We just need to practice our observation and listening skills, including our internal vision and hearing. Taking time to picture or meditate upon images of natural beauty that attract us, and allowing ourselves to see the animals and birds in our mind's eye is one way to refresh our souls.

Wildlife Imagery® is powerful medicine. In 2006, I developed it to help myself remain grounded in the face of my fears and connected to the wild beings at one with the earth. I have only to close my eyes and envision the wild guides that share their powers and abilities with me. Immediately, I am surrounded by friends I can rely on for protection. I take them with me often, and since Wildlife Imagery can be used both as a therapeutic modality and by anyone with an imagination, I have supported both clients in my practice and friends who needed a foundation for peace of mind.

Many indigenous peoples of the Americas and worldwide maintain their connections to all beings and to the understanding that all living things are interconnected and interdependent. When non-natives cut themselves off from where they originated—within the natural environments and among the animals, plants, birds, and fish—they are lost. Earth is our Source. Many of us have removed ourselves from our relationship to it, and that has caused us to struggle for balance in modern life. Welcoming guidance from those who thrive in the natural rhythms can bring peace. In my darkest moments, I call upon my Wildlife Imagery guides to show me the way, bring light to the depths, and bring power to my purpose.

Would you like to rediscover your own balance? For starters, what slice of nature could you immerse yourself in? A park nearby, a hiking trail, a bit of land with grasses and trees? If you're not near a natural area, sit quietly and imagine your favorite outdoor spot. In either case, breathe deeply while noticing the layout of the space. Carefully observe any plants, rock formations, and water sources, and just *be* in that space. You don't need to connect with any animals to start. Just be present and focus on the sights, sounds, and smells.

Eventually, your guides will show themselves. Let them know you are there only to ask for their support.

Remain breathing deeply in that natural area, in reality or in your mind, for three to five minutes. Next time, you could stay longer. (In Eastern healing methods, 36 conscious breaths are seen as being transformative. Thirty-six is another number, like 9 in the Simple Steps, that represents the end of one cycle and beginning of another). Take note of every detail you see, hear, feel, smell, and taste. Allow your senses to be awakened in this place and visit it often. These are the first steps to creating your conversations with nature, your Source. Building upon these connections to nature, wild plants and animals pull us out of the often overwhelmingly frenetic pace of our own lives and human life around us. There is nothing physically or emotionally healthful about sitting indoors for hours, staring at screens, and eating whatever we have a second to grab. Getting ourselves back outside, connecting to nature, and moving our bodies is the natural design of our existence. Going back to our Source is the remedy for peace of mind.

REFLECTION

Is there someone close to you that you cannot fully trust? Is there a painful or shocking memory of a family member's behavior that sticks with you? Have you ever been afraid of someone you love?

Who do you trust? Is there someone who has your back, who you can trust with your story? Look to animals and nature as well as people. Think about who in your trusted circle you could make a pact with to share support.

YOUR MEDITATION MANTRA

I can keep myself safe, without having to focus so much on other people's behaviors.

ACTION STEPS

Make a list in your journal of the people and animals you trust. Below each name, note any beliefs and behaviors you share with this trusted person or animal. Leave space under each entry so you can go back and add notes on how your thinking evolves as your conversations continue.

Peter the Morgan. My first trail ride ever! 1973

My memory of this day is clearer than this old photo.

3

RELATIONSHIPS

As I grew and evolved into a teenager and young woman, I observed my close friends' relationships with their parents and siblings. Certainly, these connections varied, but none looked quite like my family circus. A stark difference between my friends' homes and my own was that I had an open invitation to join them for their meals and family gatherings. I enjoyed many dinners and holiday events in these safer spaces. But I never invited friends to my house. I couldn't guess when my father was going to come home drunk and crazy, or by the time I was a teenager, whether a sibling might do the same.

Though I know any teen can feel embarrassed by their family, I was mortified by the idea of my friends seeing my personal den of dysfunction. Out of necessity, I found plenty of reasons to be away from the house whenever possible. I became masterful at hiding my anxiety, and I developed a reputation for being both confrontational and avoidant, which served to deflect attention from my obsessive thoughts and fear-based behaviors. Even today, I have to stay vigilant to avoid getting trapped in repetitive, obsessive thought patterns. And yes, it is possible to break them and end the chatter.

I was not the only one capable of hiding my inner self from others. My mom was also a master of deflection. She turned a blind eye to Alex, who was several years my senior, and Alex's friends using our garden shed, which they had plastered with black-light posters, to smoke hash and conduct other "experiments." These partners in crime would hole up in the psychedelic shed for hours and get drunk and high on a regular basis. Backyard life and gardening continued around this as if the drug den didn't exist. It was easier for my mom to avoid making Alex mad than it was to require accountability for this behavior. Unfortunately, Alex was robbed of the opportunity to learn valuable lessons that could have led to successfully managing adult life. Instead, the enabling continued, and Alex's dependence on my mom grew until she became a central focus of financial support.

The depth of my mother's denial, and whatever negative effects her actions or inactions had on others, amounted to her showing absolutely no concern. Denial was one of her coping mechanisms for her own fear and anxiety. If she couldn't or wouldn't see it, it didn't exist. In addition to cleaning, cooking, and taking care of her own children, she was wrapped up in her full-time job—while dealing with a husband who was detached at best and abusive at worst. Bothering to investigate what was up in the backyard garden shed every evening didn't make it onto her radar screen. My immediate family members all swept it under the rug and went about our business.

It was in my sophomore year of high school that I blew my cover. My health class was watching a documentary about families coping with addiction. A battered and crying teenager, drunk and injured in a car crash, flashed across the screen. I snapped. It was the first full-blown panic attack I displayed in public, and it was in front of my peers. I ran from the room, and my trusted friend Miriam followed me. She was right there to comfort and support me. Our relationship was and still is among my best evidence for confiding in someone who has your back. Had I endured that moment alone, I'm certain I would have imploded.

Like some of our ancestors and other extended family members, Alex was nursing a budding addiction, drinking and using drugs since middle school. As I approached high school and Alex reached twenty something, this relationship with alcohol and drugs became all-consuming. After becoming blind drunk on a party night, this deeply distrustful, artistic relative who had been negotiating friendship and theft with the wrong crowd wrapped body, mind, and vehicle around a telephone pole.

When my mom and I visited the hospital, Alex was a mass of cuts and broken bones, sobbing in a hospital bed surrounded by nurses. The emotional pain this young person had lived with before the accident became clear to me as the years passed. Times when Alex and I had interacted at family events were never particularly enjoyable. Alex was consistently impatient, unwelcoming, and surly toward others. I couldn't comprehend the agony that had caused the need for such self-medication, and I struggled to understand why Alex seemed to dislike me so much. Following Alex's lead, I buried my pain and confusion, and they morphed into another layer of crazymaking anxiety. My own budding disorder would require medication, though medication of a different kind. It would also require help from my friends.

Unfortunately, while continuing to enable my father's alcoholism and trying to rescue Alex, my mother attempted to save Logan from financial ruin and homelessness. Logan became dependent on my mother at every turn and antagonized anyone who dared defy her perceived superiority. While living in a nearby city in a tiny home that my mother had helped purchase, Logan began to receive property tax bills, which she didn't pay. Instead of finding a way to get these bills paid, Logan began a battle of wills with that city. It took five years for them to remove her and seize the property. When the property was reclaimed, both the mortgage money my mom had invested in it and the equity gained quickly vaporized.

Sometime later, Logan cultivated a daily connection with my mother, who was then in her early nineties. Logan began to weave designs on taking over my mother's house when she passed. Frustrated and angry with the arguments Logan would start over wanting financial control over her estate, my mother would call me to complain. All I could do was remind her that she could insist that Logan apply for aid and housing. That never happened. This relationship of codependency continued until my mother's death at age ninety-five. And because she was of sound mind up to the end and unwilling to draw boundaries with her defiant relative, I was power-less to block Logan's crazymaking coup to control my mom's house and estate until after she died.

REFLECTION

What have you been hiding away that you could "share and air" with a trusted friend? What burden might you think too heavy to put upon another? When has an animal or human friend truly been there for you? And when have you taken the opportunity to be a safe harbor and support for another?

YOUR MEDITATION MANTRA

To be a friend to others, I must first be a friend to myself.

ACTION STEPS

This page in your journal will be divided into two columns. Title one column "Characteristics of a Trusted Friend" and list the characteristics that a friend you could trust would have. Title the second column "My Own Characteristics" and note the characteristics you possess that a friend can depend on. Add to these lists as you observe yourself and your relationships more closely.

Sunday Morning with Miriam. 1994

4

MEDICATION

Antidepressants are designed to alleviate anxiety and depression. For a year and a half, I took Lexapro with the belief that it might improve my brain's healthy serotonin function. I hoped for it to reset whatever had gone off-kilter and made me so anxious all the time. It was during a spell when I felt unsafe riding horses that I decided to try it. Not being able to ride with confidence was a deal-breaker.

I never intended to take any medication long-term. Antidepressants often work very effectively, but since all drugs have side effects, I was concerned about extended use. Lexapro's side effects are few and I tolerated it quite well. As advertised, it did increase my overall sense of well-being and reduced my nervousness. Still, any drug has effects beyond what it is intended to treat.

During that time, I began to study and learn much about nutrition and hydration. I stopped eating gluten and limited my dairy intake. Whole foods like fresh vegetables, fruits, grains, and lean meats immediately gave me more clarity. I began to avoid fast food and processed food, both of which made me feel edgy; I bought organic food whenever possible and tried to keep sugar to a minimum. I was finally diagnosed with celiac sprue after seeing a gastroenterologist and requesting that test. Having eliminated gluten from my diet and eating a much higher percentage of plant-based and organic foods, I slowly weaned myself from the Lexapro, which I eliminated after about eighteen months.

Among the most powerful medications to calm my anxiety was (and continues to be) time spent in nature and in the company of horses, dogs, and barn cats. Animal energy was easy for me to understand, and they could interact with me while maintaining their own special dignity and wisdom. Because pets and wildlife were unfailingly honest, my trust in them was complete. The more relationships I built with animals, the more trusting I became. By that time, the frequency of my panic attacks had decreased greatly, but the struggle with anxiety continued.

When my spinning thoughts threatened to overpower me, I put on my running shoes. I loved running. I ran and ran. At dawn and at night. In the humid heat, the cold, and the pouring rain. Legs churning, I blew through neighborhood streets, burning my angst behind me. I didn't have a tendency toward addiction to alcohol or drugs, but I had become addicted to anxiety, and I knew that running was like medicine to me. Movement provided relief, and I soon became a fitness instructor and avid hiker.

Movement is still medicine for me. These days, I spend a lot of time in Pilates practice and outdoors, walking dogs and hiking with my horse as much as I ride him. For me, there is no substitute for moving my body when my mind gets stuck. Newton's First Law of Motion says that an object in motion tends to stay in motion, which is why I remain physically fit and able. And to this day, my time spent with animals and moving in nature is when I am most grounded and at peace.

Like the visions of Charlotte the spider I conjured as a child, my imagination moved more and more toward my development of Wildlife Imagery as a therapeutic modality, and my mind became quieter. I practice Wildlife Imagery as personal therapy every day, and I incorporate it in support of others. It has allowed me to access the power, grace, and flexibility I need to keep my balance and remain positive. Any time I need support, especially when there is no trusted human available who can be there for me in difficult times, I surround myself with images of my wildlife guides and ask for their leadership to set me back on the right path. I focus on their powers and strengths to lead me through whatever difficulty I am experiencing. This meditation medication comes with only positive side effects. When I sit quietly by myself and call my wildlife guides to me, I ask for their protection and insight. They always arrive with the guidance I need to move forward.

Over the years of practice, I have developed a core group of six wildlife guides who are always with me. There is Wolf for protection, Horse for grace and power, Dragonfly for allowing transformation, Bighorn Sheep to help me reach new heights, Hawk to show me the greater picture, and Snake to clear the path ahead of me. In any circumstance in which I need to ground myself or ask for any of their assistance, I need only to stop, bring up the images of them in my mind, and breathe deeply. I ask for their support in any challenging situation. Adding the intentional breathing quiets my thoughts and allows me to tune into their guidance. I am immediately calmed, and I feel surrounded by supportive friends.

Certainly, there are times when conventional medications can be helpful. And I did experience a period of their use, with good results. I kept in mind my goal to use Lexapro only temporarily, while I made healthful lifestyle changes and incorporated movement and

Wildlife Imagery practice as main aids to reduce anxiety. Getting outdoors to release pent-up energy and knowing my six wildlife friends are always with me when I need support is powerful medicine, indeed.

REFLECTION

What pains have you endured for which you've been prescribed or invented medications? Which of your self-medication options is safe to practice? Are there unhealthy choices or addictions you've been caught up in to hide that part of you that feels out of control? How do you respond to the desire to numb out or just feel more peaceful?

YOUR MEDITATION MANTRA

I can choose healthful alternatives to increase my inner peace.

ACTION STEPS

Look back through your journal for actions, situations, or time periods during which your desire to medicate is strongest. (Keeping a separate paper calendar where you can record what triggers you and when you're triggered may help you see patterns and ground your memory). As this section of your journal grows, look for habits in your reactions. Take note of specific relationships, duties, days, or times that feel repeatedly triggering and in which you want to be soothed. Note which choices you've made for self-soothing.

Greeting a Friend at Mission: Wolf. Gardner, CO. 1998

5

DARKNESS

Though their education was limited to high school, my parents were naturally intelligent and capable. They did not receive or apparently value higher education, so when it was time for me to consider life after high school, I didn't have a personal vision of continuing education. Fortunately, the parents of my closest friends were educated people who cared about me. Their support and the ways they challenged my personal limiting beliefs were a true gift. They spoke the truth to me about my intelligence and abilities.

I was inspired by this, and it was a saving grace when my mom's reaction to my announcement that I intended to go to college was to discourage me. She was threatened by the possibility that I'd become "all smart and not talk to the rest of the family." It was a hit, for sure, but by this time I was accustomed to her attacks on my self-confidence. I chose to recognize the positivity that the precious adults outside my family reflected back to me. Fortunately, my mom did come around to the idea that I was bound for higher education and was ready and willing to drive me to Connecticut from Massachusetts when the time came to move into my college dorm.

The first few months of college were filled with new friendships and experiences. It was a dream come true. I loved being in a program for equine studies and business. My vision of opening a horse boarding or training facility had a pulse. Unfortunately, so did my anxiety. It bloomed and blossomed, and the freedom I had felt in this new environment turned to a death by a thousand cuts. First, I would show up late for some classes or leave early, telling myself it was no big deal. Then, there were the multiple trips to the bathroom during classes to catch my breath and try to slow my heart rate. And later, the thought of leaving my dorm would trigger my panic attacks. Just attending classes and riding the shuttle to the training barn soon became impossible. I had no idea that this pattern was the classic development of agoraphobia.

The doors that had opened for me became walls closing in. I was eighteen years old. Having been raised in a family where no one sought or valued education beyond high school and being unable to see myself as any different, I lacked confidence and thought the odds of my achieving a college degree were slim. No one at home, including me, expected I'd do much more than take a low-level job and wait for a husband to come along. But I did have a love for learning and the emotional support of a few trusted adults. I had survived the chaos of my childhood and moved beyond the assumption by a high school counselor that I was not exactly college material.

When I received word of my acceptance into the college of my choice and began my higher education, I thought I was finally free. Free of the constraints of my small town. Free of family dysfunction. Free of the torturous thoughts in my head as I tried to establish healthy relationships. Free of fear and debilitating anxiety. Free of the crazymakers.

I could not have been more wrong.

That December felt like the end for me because I couldn't imagine myself dropping out of college after my first semester, but that's exactly what happened. With the help of my friends' parents, I had come to see myself as intelligent and worthy of successfully achieving a college degree. I expected to engage in learning and use my new skills to move myself into a career surrounded by the animals that had saved my sanity. Instead, now unable to attend classes and trapped again, I saw no option but to return home.

Talk about crazymaking! Anxiety was the death knell for my first college experience. And because this was before my initial mental health diagnosis and treatment, I was certain I was losing my mind. My worst nightmare had come true. I'd be heading home to live with my mother and her boyfriend. It was the lowest point of my life, and I wasn't sure I could continue. The anxiety beasts haunted me round the clock. I hardly slept at all and became depressed with exhaustion. I frequently sat alone and wrote bad poetry about death and suicide. Those days were dark indeed.

At least my few close friends didn't give up on me, and though they didn't understand what was wrong, they pulled me out of my funk as much as possible. My class clown friend Heidi was always able to make me laugh, either at her expense or mine. What a gift that was (and still is).

For a while, I took a job at a local grocery store. I didn't know how to get out of my situation, but the achiever and the survivor in me were determined to find a way. I went to work as a checkout clerk and tried to breathe. After clocking in, I'd head for the register, push grocery items over the scanner, and smile at customers. My brain went on autopilot and disconnected me from my experience. Customers were greeted. Money was counted. Groceries were bagged. The predictability of my days was welcomed but soon became constraining.

Somehow, the drive for education—the one thing I knew I could excel at if I could stay grounded—showed its face again. It came knocking at my door when a friend suggested I consider the veterinary technician program at our local agricultural college. Since that program at least involved daily contact with animals, I threw myself into classes and the care of the dogs and cats on the ward. I could negotiate that small world for a while.

Pretty soon, a trainer from my previous horse life came calling. He said the polo barn in the next town needed management help. I went back to work with horses. Animals in general, and horses in particular, had always made much more sense to me than most people, and a horse barn was a place in which I felt completely at peace. Just like Fern in *Charlotte's Web*, I loved everything about the times I spent in horse barns. I had only to drive or bike from my home to the lavish stable in the next town to care for the horses and hounds each day.

I kept my head down, stayed out of the social drama that often surrounds such bastions of entitlement as fox hunting and polo stables, and felt sure I'd be all right.

But these were days when I began to experience a lot of physical pain in my work, and my digestive system was mounting an all-out war. I felt constantly bloated and achy. Back pain became a daily visitor, so I found a local chiropractor to x-ray my spine, and my journey into scoliosis treatment began. Cue the crazymakers. I was referred to a specialist, fitted with a brace, and told it was unwise for me to keep riding horses or ever consider having children.

The specter of anxiety stalked me constantly, and its shadow loomed ever larger with each day. I was able to feel safe only at home, as crazy as it was, and at the barn. Everywhere else, I felt trapped and afraid people would discover that I was barely functional. My mind was constantly spinning with the fear that my craziness would be discovered. The panic attacks I dealt with almost daily were pulling me deeper into agoraphobia, where I would soon be unable to move.

It all came to a head when one lovely fall day when I was unable to leave my home to return to work after a lunch break. I was paralyzed with fear. It had piled up and up until the weight of it was too much. I had become trapped in the house despite the crazymaking energy I lived with there, because I could no longer tolerate the feeling of being unable to move about freely in the outside world, even for seconds and in everyday situations. Being stopped in traffic, standing in line to check out groceries, closed in a plane or elevator, or waiting for customer service at the bank—any public place or social gathering in which I could not easily escape undetected—became impossible for me to bear.

And the stress. The exhausting, haunting, paranoid stress. This hostile takeover of my life by agoraphobia could have kept me homebound for years, but resourcefulness and resilience saved me. I wasn't stuck at home long before I made the decision to get help. It marked the beginning of finding my way out of my inner crazymaking.

REFLECTION

Have there been events, relationships, or situations in which anxiety has robbed you of what you hold dear? Have you said no to attractive invitations because you were afraid you might be embarrassed or have a panic attack? In what ways, small and large, has anxiety altered the course of your life?

Who is available to support you, outside of the family that raised you? Who have you allowed to know your inner self enough to ask for their support? Have you accessed any professional resources?

YOUR MEDITATION MANTRA

In my darkest moments, I will reach out for support instead of hiding my pain.

ACTION STEPS

If you don't feel ready to tell someone about the roots of your anxiety, write a letter in your journal to yourself or someone else. You don't need to send it. Note what you believe anxiety has stolen from you. Go back another day and circle the one or two most costly important events, relationships, or situations you'd like to return to and have a do-over with your new ability. Sketch some notes about what you would change in your behavior to make those situations better. Take this one small step at a time. Give yourself the grace to examine one habit or behavior that you'd like to improve upon. Spending time picturing yourself in a new situation in which you can make better choices can lead you to making them a reality.

College Graduation, Take 2. June 1995

6

GUTS

When I left college and returned home angry and hopeless, I reconnected with a toxic ex-boyfriend. It was as if I wanted to punish myself further. At that point, my digestive system simply shut down. I was an otherwise fit nineteen-year-old when I was first hospitalized with intestinal blockage and rectal bleeding.

That began a long road of testing that, sadly, did not include evaluation for a gluten allergy or sensitivity, though gluten had been on the IBS (irritable bowel syndrome) radar for years. For me, IBS had become a true horror show. On a suggestion from a coworker, I found a gastroenterologist and had myself tested for what was mostly still pooh-poohed in 2002: celiac disease. It's a chronic digestive and immune disorder that damages the small intestine, and it's triggered by eating foods containing gluten. I had been floundering in the medical community for twenty years with severe symptoms of IBS, and no doctor had ever suggested that I be tested for celiac.

Twenty years.

It is only recently that many restaurants and some food manufacturers offer gluten-free options. Incorporating and working with ingredients that contain no gluten is often more expensive, making it difficult for people with sensitivities to avoid them. The sources of gluten proteins are wheat, rye, and barley. And wheat flour is found in many products that would surprise you. In addition to the obvious breads, cookies, cakes, and pies, some candies and many sauces contain gluten.

In some people, gluten can destroy the lining of the small intestine, which normally contains flexible villi.

Villi look like tiny waving fingers that help move food along its course. In untreated celiac disease, these villi can be destroyed, leaving the small intestine less able to allow absorption of critical nutrients. With testing and diagnosis of celiac still not a forefront consideration of physicians worldwide, many people suffer needlessly, both with physical symptoms of this autoimmune disorder and high levels of anxiety and distress. And the connections between anxiety with gluten sensitivity and celiac disease are well-documented in scientific research. As a result, these many years later, I have been 100 percent gluten free and manage celiac well. I was gluten free before gluten free was cool!

If your gut is performing poorly, or you are struggling to understand why you feel anxious, or both, you might want to insist on tests for gluten sensitivity and celiac disease. They are not the same, but both can cause you significant physical and emotional distress.

Since anxiety often shows itself in diseases of the gut, more investigation of my issues began with a glucose tolerance test. If you have a soda addiction, this will cure it. Drinking a thick orange "soda" many times sweeter than the bottled versions was enough to turn me away from regular sodas for good. And then the barium "milkshake" and enema were next. Barium looked like ice cream, but the taste was pretty awful. And an enema was not my idea of a good time. Through this research, I discovered I was hypoglycemic (low blood sugar), but that was it. A simple blood test for celiac sprue would have changed my life.

All this medical intervention and testing was not targeted to what I actually needed, which was comprehensive nutrition testing combined with good, solid mental health intervention. It turns out I had to give up all gluten, cow dairy, eggs, almonds, bananas, and several lesser food irritants. I felt much better when I gave up the foods causing me distress. Neither nutrition nor mental health were mentioned to me during all the testing, and no referrals were made. They both may have saved me many more years of severe anxiety and poor digestive function.

If you have explored neither gluten sensitivity nor comprehensive nutrition testing, I suggest you start right away. Your suffering could be greatly reduced just by getting tested for gluten sensitivity, celiac disease, or other food sensitivities. And knowing your real nutritional needs will allow you to do something about them. Doing this research could save you a lot of time, money, and bad tasting "treats" like barium.

My body has put up with a lot. And I ask a whole lot of it these days with ranch chores, Pilates, hiking, and strength training. And never mind managing work and relationship stress every day. Balancing all of this with getting enough truly restful sleep and relaxation can be a real challenge. It is also a daily goal for me. Despite all the energy I had concentrated on my mental health, I didn't give up on my quest to also heal my physical self.

Your body is resilient too, and the better you can treat it, the more comfort and joy it will give back to you. The mind-body is one, and integrating your self-care on both levels can give you the freedom to enjoy your relationships and activities while feeling more energized and happier. The body, with its web of meridians carrying the flow of energy and helping to keep all its systems functioning well, is a true temple. It is a sacred gift to be nourished and cherished.

Speaking of meridians, the web of energy pathways throughout your body, I have had the privilege of training in EFT (Emotional Freedom Techniques) with the Association for Comprehensive Energy Psychology. EFT draws on the traditional Chinese medicine practice of acupressure and adds in the brain hemisphere stimulation of EMDR (Eye Movement Desensitization and Reprocessing) while the person being treated talks about challenges. It is amazingly effective and brings fast results. I have found it very helpful in managing my anxiety and in supporting others. Tapping on the meridians to release stuck energy while engaging in supportive talk therapy makes for a powerful combination to help you to release the blocks caused by negative emotions and traumas.

It takes guts to examine your poorly functioning guts. More than a few folks have endured serious digestive illnesses and cancers because it's uncomfortable and scary to uncover why we might be feeling poorly. And when emotional blocks and traumatic memories stay stuck in us, that stress can certainly add to digestive dysfunction. Know that feeding your body with good nutrition and avoiding processed foods and sugary drinks can keep your gut healthy. When addressing any issues, it's important to advocate for yourself when you can feel there's a problem and it isn't being properly addressed. Go with your gut when anything feels off.

REFLECTION

The gut tells us how well the mind-body is functioning. What physical symptoms have you noticed that you might connect to anxiety and stress? Abdominal pain? Constipation? Diarrhea? Rashes? Headaches? Irritability? Do you have other physical ailments for which you've found no explanation? Have you stopped taking physical care of yourself as a result of the anxiety you are experiencing?

YOUR MEDITATION MANTRA

When there seems to be no solution to my mental or physical distress, I will keep searching for answers and advocating for myself.

ACTION STEPS

You may want to list what you eat each day and record how you feel afterward. Call your doctor and make an appointment to rule out gluten sensitivity and celiac disease. Though the symptoms are most often gastrointestinal (constipation and diarrhea are common), they can also show up as anxiety, attention disorders, chronic skin irritations, mood swings, and headaches. You could try EFT or EMDR by connecting with a therapist who offers them. Some therapists even offer these practices online, and they are effective. The positive results you could experience may surprise you.

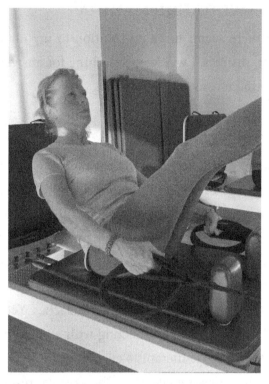

Keeping up my core strength with Pilates. 2023

7

CLEANING HOUSE

My late twenties to mid-thirties were spent working on my first entrepreneurial endeavor, a storefront and contract-based uniform supply business. I hid the specter of my anxiety behind hard work and a twisted sense of humor. Avoiding crowds was mostly possible, though I did find myself caught at times. Movie theaters and concerts were still out of range, but with a military veteran boyfriend with his own trauma-related fears, this worked . . . for a while.

It was during this phase that I began commuting to a nearby college for an undergraduate degree in

psychology. At this point, I was the "elder" in a continuing education sector that offered a support program for
single mothers. A professor invited me to co-author a
study of this program with her, which gave me some
confidence in my abilities as a student and budding
mental health professional. Besides that uplifting opportunity, I learned a lot about psychology in general, but
not much about myself.

More real education came to me in the form of an
internship at the Veterans Administration Outpatient
Clinic in Boston, MA. The men in whose group therapy
sessions I participated or with whom I tried to learn to
shoot pool were an education in themselves. Most dealt
with unfathomable trauma and negative connections
to the legal system. Some were on the edge of incarcer-
ation, and others were like lost kids looking for acceptance. Being invited to know each of them in even the
smallest ways was a privilege. And it was a true joy to see
them reach out for connection as they began to rebuild
self-confidence.

Even traveling to and from this VA clinic was therapeutic for me, if exhausting. It was an opportunity to work through the enormous challenge of riding the train in and out of the city from the northern suburbs. With few strategies for managing my anxiety, I'd arrive at the clinic feeling like I'd already run a marathon, while others would show up relaxed from gazing out at the world passing by the windows or reading a book. It was my first experience with a practice-in-the-setting therapeutic technique, though I was my only support.

Beginning to understand my own psychological foundation came with my first connection with a wonderful psychologist. I picked him from my health plan's list because he was male and had a happy sounding name, Dr Richard Fitzpatrick. And since I didn't trust men after such negative connections with my father, one brother, some boyfriends, and a couple of narcissistic and sexist male bosses, I figured building a relationship with a healthy, balanced man might be a good idea.

Connecting with Rich turned out to be a pivotal decision in my life. What he helped me to understand about my emotions, my limiting beliefs, and my family influence was *profound*. He looked a bit like a blue-eyed leprechaun and often sat with his feet propped up on his desk, drinking a soda or munching a candy bar. Hardly the image of the stuffy, note-writing questioner of my imagination, this thoughtful man knew how to meet me just where I was at the age of twenty-something, and he made an absolute difference for me. Rich helped me identify my emotions, trust myself, and be a much better detective in my personal relationships.

Among the important lessons and strategies I learned in my therapeutic relationship with Rich and from other helpful professionals and healing methods was that relationships need occasional house cleaning. Most of us have some connections to others that are healthy and in our best interest. And it seems there is always a crazy-making relationship or two that may be unwise or even unsafe. Especially when it comes to family, it can be very hard to maintain clarity about whether the relationship is healthy or maybe damaging to you.

Often, people make excuses for family members who treat them poorly. Or they try to ignore being put down, shut up, or used for emotional target practice. When it comes to family relationships, guilt shows up and makes you question your right to preserve your own safety and dignity.

Of course, it's always best when you can discuss and move forward from differences that arise with your family members. Occasionally though, a familial relationship can become so toxic and irreparable that you need to remove yourself from it to maintain your own sanity. It is particularly crazymaking when relationship difficulties are generational—when they are hatched in broken connections and issues among the people who came before you and become a miserable inheritance.

As I entered my thirties, Chris, another family member my mom was fearful of alienating, went into a crazymaking tailspin that no one saw coming. Without explanation, Chris asked several of us for money, and friends began to report concerns for the safety of the kids in this branch of the family.

Predictably enough, my mom didn't want to rock the boat and risk rejection by any family member, immediate or extended, so she was at a loss when there were requests made for significant amounts of money. While I was at work at my retail business in town and busy working toward my degree in psychology, my mom dropped by unannounced. She begged me to meet with Chris's concerned friends at her house sometime later, to figure out what to do. Oh, I thought, here it comes! I'm being dragged into this crazymaking drama I have nothing to do with, because the older adults involved are at a loss for how to respond. Everyone appeared to be afraid of creating an explosion.

With a pit in my stomach, I arrived at my mom's house that evening to find the friend group sitting at the table. Chris's requests for money and other surprising behaviors were enough for this group to be gathering at my mother's house and wringing their hands about what to do. Of course, I was dragged into it by my mom in the hopes that I'd take the fall for her by taking action. Unfortunately, her plan worked.

After witnessing much circle talk and handwringing about what action to take, I'd had enough. Rolling my eyes and backing out of the room, I said, "Fine. I'll do something if all you can do is talk." Based on the dramatic discussion, what I did was call social services and make a report since the safety of minors appeared to be at stake, and that was enough to motivate me to act. Though reports are supposed to be confidential, I received a call from Chris, threatening to kill me. Lesson learned from the crazymakers! The generational garbage that I had nothing to do with was laid at my feet for me to step in once again.

Some weeks later, while watching the local paper for my name to appear on the list of 1995 honors graduates at my college, I was faced again with the death of my brother, Tomar, and the painfully public details about Chris. Announcements about them appeared together in our local newspaper, on the same day— Tomar's for the obituary I wrote after he died from AIDS and Chris's for being arrested for embezzling tens of thousands of dollars from a neighbor. It was a crazymaking double-whammy. I was crushed to lose my vital relationship with Tomar, but I was powerless against his terminal illness. My relationship with Chris and several relatives in that family branch, while never close, had clearly ended.

Your potential decision to end a toxic friendship or dysfunctional familial relationship may be met with criticism and shame from loved ones. But only you can know the intimate details of your connections. Consulting a mental health professional with whom you can review and reflect on the specifics of any relationship can help you create the boundaries you need to care for yourself. Ultimately, your personal peace and overall safety are most important.

It is often said that blood is thicker than water. And while anyone would be glad to have positive, loving relationships with immediate and extended family, in some cases that just isn't possible. For those of us who have endured painful relationships with family members, the choice to release ourselves if we feel unsafe is appropriate. Building our own families by making deep friendship connections can be equally valuable and essential. Whether your trusted allies are blood or water, you deserve to be among loved ones who support you in healthy ways that help you thrive.

REFLECTION

What feelings arise when you think of the important relationships in your life? Can you see relationships in which your safety may be at stake? How would you assess your own growth in your relationships with others?

Are there relationships from which you need to back off? If you realized that was true and you did some house cleaning, why did you? If you pushed those relationship problems out of your mind or chose to not act on them, why did you make that choice?

YOUR MEDITATION MANTRA

All my relationships have helped me to grow. I will look for the gift in each one and hold fast to those in which I am accepted unconditionally.

ACTION STEPS

Take stock of how your perception has grown. In your journal, make a list of your relationships with family, friends, neighbors, coworkers, and pets. Next to each, note realizations you've had about your growth in relation to these others. If no realizations of growth come to mind, make a note next to the relationships in which you'd like to make improvements or do some house cleaning. Also, letting those with whom you have positive relationships know how much you appreciate them can preserve those connections. Sending a quick note, text, or voicemail to express your thanks could be an enormous boost to someone who has shown you kindness.

Learn to be done. Not mad, not bothered. Just done. Protect your peace at all costs.

Self-protection. Start today!

8

PERSEVERANCE

The path of my recovery from panic disorder, agoraphobia, and social anxiety is lined with horses—beautiful, powerful, intelligent, graceful horses. I could write volumes about the horses in my life and the effects they've had on me. I'm grateful for the many hours I've spent sitting in the corners of their stalls, watching and listening to them peacefully munching hay and blowing their warm breath on my hands. Like Fern in *Charlotte's Web*, I love everything about being in a barn. It's truly my happy place.

The weaving of horses throughout my life has been a barometer of sorts for my levels of anxiety. Always, the horses bring me back to myself, to their care, and to the necessity of being grounded to function in their presence. And when I have been unable to ride because I've been too anxious and not able to lead, the desire to get back to a place of balance where I could again sit calmly in the saddle has been an ever-present driving force in my life.

Even the one time I was seriously injured when riding was not enough to make me quit. Trotting through a field with a group of friends, I noticed one of them was having trouble with a young paint mare that I had been exercising for her. The horse appeared to be about to buck my friend off, so I traded horses with her. After unsaddling the mare and inspecting her body and equipment for signs of something amiss, I could find nothing wrong. I put her saddle back on, checked that all was correct, and mounted up.

We continued the ride for a short while. Then the mare suddenly reared up—way up. It was such an odd sensation to feel her mane in my face as I instinctively leaned forward to stay on. As quickly as she reared, she dove headfirst and started bucking with all her might. When I saw the daylight shining under my butt, time stood still. I knew I was going off. I was flung into the air and landed on my hip. Hard. As I hit the ground, I wiggled my toes. The thought that I'd live to walk and ride another day was immediately foremost in my mind. Unable to stand, however, I soon found myself in an ambulance headed to the hospital. I wound up with a partially crushed vertebra and three broken ribs. Though my injuries were serious, I recovered fully after outpatient surgery and a few months of healing. The idea of getting back on a horse, though, was pretty scary.

Fortunately, a friend who ran a therapeutic riding program had just the remedy for my fear of getting back in the saddle: a horse named Peanut. He was a sweet, old, half-blind horse who had packed little kids around for years. I started riding again on the back of this equine angel in an arena full of soft sand. It took months of practice for me to be able to ride out on trails again and feel safe, but dependable horses, horse people, and baby steps got me there.

It's not everyone who has the desire to climb on the back of a thousand-pound nervous rabbit that travels at great speed and has the ability for unexpected vertical action. It isn't for everyone. So, it's a true testament to my commitment to regain my psychic and physical balance that I can once again enjoy time in the saddle. But one horse stands out among the rest.

I've enjoyed the true privilege of having a horse named Manchi for the past seventeen years. He is a compact, black-and-white and spotted Tennessee Walking Horse gelding. Everywhere we go, people remark on how sleek and handsome he is. Manchi is about the keenest horse I have ever met. He is generally attuned to every nuance of his environment, including my emotional state. Now at the age of twenty-seven and still active, he challenges me to be the best person I can be, every day.

Manchi requires me to earn my position as his leader whenever we are together. In the horse world, every relationship is a hierarchy. One is always dominant over or subordinate to the next in a herd of horses. In the herd of two—one horse and one human—the hierarchy remains, and if the human is not able to calmly lead, the horse will take over the dominant position.

Some days it takes perseverance just to show up and do all the work required for Manchi's care. And when he tests me with subtle behaviors that need corrections, it can feel like a chore. At times like these I wonder what it might have been like for him to persevere through life with three previous owners and one who referred to him as "the devil horse." I imagine he may have been difficult to handle if treated unfairly. He keeps me on my toes and requires me to examine how I communicate with him. To say this horse has been among my greatest teachers doesn't begin to explain it.

As my daily equine educator and friend these many years, Manchi has guided me forward, grounded me in earth energy, and tested me on every level. At times when I have been stressed and anxious, Manchi has stood by me, quietly breathing his warm, soft breath over me to let me know I am still okay. Other times, he has challenged me by pushing my buttons as a rider. When I have lost confidence, he has pushed me to the far edge of fear by spooking and threatening to bolt. Manchi looks for ways to test me as his trustworthy leader, which he seeks and deserves.

My only option in maintaining this wonderful connection to my horse has been to persevere through fear and find balance again. When I have been at my most anxious and least able to remain grounded, Manchi has tested my leadership by refusing to allow me to remain in charge. He has made me look deep within myself and dig to my core to come up with the consistent follow-through to be worthy of leading him. For this, I am truly grateful.

Life offers us many opportunities to push through or give up, to find motivation or back off and hide. I take many lessons from my horse but also from nature all around us. Despite constant pressure put on them by humans, animals and plants continue to thrive, to benefit us, to offer us the opportunity to reach back and reconnect with our wild Source. Their abilities to endure give us examples to find our own way forward every day.

REFLECTION

When have you needed to dig deeper than you thought possible to get through, to survive, to shine? When have those whom you report to or lead challenged you and pushed your boundaries? Maybe you have asked yourself, "Am I accomplishing what matters? Does this person or animal see me as a qualified leader? What is my definition of a good leader? Are those who have some authority over me recognizing my strengths and abilities? Who or what is important enough for you to persevere through setbacks to make good things happen? Can I handle all of this? Am I good enough?" If you have asked yourself questions like these, spend some time reflecting on your answers. If you have not considered these thoughts, take a moment to give them a try, and identify the driving forces in your life.

YOUR MEDITATION MANTRA

Challenges will continue to test me, and I will maintain my balance as I carry on. I will persevere.

ACTION STEPS

Discuss your feelings of self-doubt with a trusted friend or animal. Label a page in your journal with "Perseverance." You don't need to be in a relationship with horses to explore the places you can dig deep to get through. Any person or animal with whom you have a positive relationship deserves your best efforts to interact.

List the relationships in which you find challenges, and for the next week, write one detail each day describing your behavior within that relationship. When the week is complete, go back and look over your notes. Highlight the details that show the behaviors you want to maintain and grow. Circle the details of your behavior that you feel need work. In the margin, note what actions you can take to persevere through the trials that arise as you alter your behaviors.

Manchi and Me. June, 2022

9

OPPORTUNITIES

When it came to the dating game, I followed my parents' patterns in intimate relationships. I picked emotionally unavailable, unhappy cads who were narcissistic and unfaithful. The connections I blindly made mirrored the same misery that my parents felt with each other and within themselves. Unless you have grown up with it, it's hard to grasp why people sometimes stay in abusive relationships and become accustomed to coping with domestic violence. As difficult as these inappropriate relationships are to navigate, the generational habit of choosing them can be hard to break. Until we can experience a new reality—or one is modeled for us—we tend to gravitate toward connections that are familiar and that we know how to navigate, even if they are very unhealthy. Having learned how to live with what I understood to be "normal," it was easy for me to fall into the same trap my family of origin set for me.

In one relationship that lasted several years, I went repeatedly to a local bar to extricate a drunk and particularly self-involved boyfriend of several years to ensure that he made it home unaccompanied by other women and without incident. It took a while to outgrow the need for self-torture that I allowed him to inflict on me.

I held onto that toxic relationship longer than I should have. It fed my addiction to anxiety and kept it at the forefront of my existence. The daily drama fueled my flawed self-image and stoked the flames of my panic attacks. At that time in my life, I was incapable of visualizing myself in a loving and respectful relationship, and my choices and actions reflected what I had learned at home.

Fortunately, this was not to be a chain around my neck forever. After several exhausting years, that unhealthy relationship finally ended in crazymaking drama while he and I were on vacation in Jamaica. Apparently, he hadn't really wanted to go there with me, most likely because, like my mom's behavior, he had just begun a new affair. There was much tension between us, and we argued loudly in our hotel room. Though it was a trip I had worked hard to earn at my travel agent job, it was clear we couldn't enjoy that vacation together.

When he said we were going home early, I felt a bubble burst in my mind. For the first time, I looked at him as a complete and dangerous stranger. There was no way I would go anywhere with him, ever again. I was *finally done*. I was done with being lied to, disrespected, and used. I bid him goodbye and stayed in Jamaica by myself, in blissful solitude by the beach, for the last few days. I enjoyed the calming waves and bird songs, several pina coladas, and a peace I had never before experienced.

Upon returning home, my peace of mind was interrupted by an unexpected visit from my now ex-boyfriend. He was enraged over my refusal to return to our dysfunctional relationship and his power over me. This final meeting ended with him screaming obscenities at me and breaking the windshield of my car. It was the most violent behavior I'd ever seen from him, but had I allowed myself to clearly acknowledge his intense reactions to previous frustrations in our relationship, I could have predicted such a blowup. It was an important lesson.

After a while, I met other men, dated, and had a relationship or two of some length. My progress was slow, but each relationship was better than the last. With each new partner, it seemed I learned a new life skill or had a new realization that helped me determine which connections were safe for me and which weren't. The hours, weeks, months, and years I spent in various types of therapy and coaching relationships were paying off.

Benefits came from individual and group talk therapy, practicing breath work in settings that sparked my anxiety, being medicated for a year and a half, meditating with Sufis, and even an attempt at whirling with dervishes. I consulted an intuitive about my life's path and my relationships and began spending time reconnecting my deepest self to nature and listening quietly in the presence of horses. I released traumatic memories with EMDR and opened blocked energy pathways through EFT with tapping. With every healing opportunity that presented itself to me, I learned something more about life and about myself. My understanding of my own fractured feelings and reactions grew clearer, and my radar for detecting liars and cheats was sharpened. I began to attract kinder, more respectful men who were interested in my success and happiness.

Finally, in 1994, I met my husband, Scott, who is one of the kindest, friendliest, and most loving men I know. When we fell into a companionable silence near the end of our drive home on our second date, I knew I had finally arrived at my safe place. It was an adjustment for me to accept being loved unconditionally and to understand that he was as interested in my self-fulfillment as he was in his own. Negotiating these new waters was worth it, for sure. Never have I questioned his support and love. They are ever-present.

While this may sound like a "happily ever after" wrap-up, it's not. And while it would be great to anticipate that the crazymakers of my anxiety must have packed their bags and moved on, that's not exactly what happened.

In 1999, I was diagnosed with early-stage melanoma on my back. Being very light-skinned and having spent summers on New England beaches, I was in for a long haul with skin cancer. That first life-threatening diagnosis came in the form of a phone call at work from my dermatologist. I felt as if the floor under me had dropped away. Cue a new crazymaking layer of anxiety! I was very fortunate that the tiny melanoma was treatable and removable. It prompted me to write a short story titled *The Melon Baller* because that was what it felt like to have the necessary margins scooped out to protect me from the melanoma spreading further.

Life went on, my health remained steady, and I began pursuing a master's degree in education. I became a middle school teacher and a fitness instructor, both of which kept me very busy. As much as possible, I spent time in the horse world, met new horse people, and continued riding, mostly on horses that had been rejected or ignored by their humans and needed exercise and attention.

Despite experiencing some continuing struggles with panic attacks when confined in planes, elevators, movie theaters and the like, I had the great fortune of a solid marriage. Like me, Scott enjoyed the outdoors and animals. Our decision to move west to Colorado was a real test of my self-confidence, and it required me to dig deep for the inner strength to go through with it. Packing up and leaving the places and people that had defined my 30-plus years was challenging and lonely at first. It was also freeing to leave behind much of the painful history of my earlier life. Soon, some time spent in the mountains and near the many horses and equine activities available to me confirmed that I had made the right move.

As Scott and I began building our life together in our new home, I turned to the power of wildlife to help heal myself. I wasn't aware then of the depth of the guidance I had received so long ago from the famous literary spider, Charlotte, my first Wildlife Imagery mentor. But I knew I had always been happier around animals and in nature than anywhere else. I came to appreciate the power and grace that Horse had shown me as I recovered from the debilitating level of anxiety I had lived with for decades. And the grounding and protection I had always received from the dogs in my life came to me in the vision of Wolf.

Soon, Wolf and Horse became the wildlife guides whose images I turned to for comfort in human-dominated situations that triggered my anxiety. I realized that they could accompany me and offer me support anywhere and at any time. I had only to ask for them to appear. Since then, four other wildlife guides have become my constant companions:

Dragonfly, Bighorn Sheep, Hawk, and Snake. I call upon all these friends daily to help me negotiate the world in which we live.

It was a good thing that I was soon steeped in Wildlife Imagery self-care because an MRI of my spine became necessary. I began to develop pain in my mid back that just wouldn't quit. Prior to my riding accident, I had been a frequent runner. Mine was a life filled with movement and fitness. Having to give up running after the spinal injury was a blow, but I soon made other choices to stay fit: Pilates, lots of dog walking, and strength training. This was working well until I began to have back pain while horseback riding. Having never had an MRI, I discovered that it is about the most claustrophobic, noisy, and time-consuming test there is. How was I going to manage this without drugs for sedation? It was possible only with my wildlife guides.

Horse and Wolf accompanied me through that awful MRI experience. In my vision, one stood on each side of me and close to my face. They offered me their strength, power, grace, and protection. I imagined my hands touching them as I conversed with them, asking them to help me stay in the tube and not panic. Combined with the alert buzzer the attendant gave me to hold in case I suddenly needed to be pulled out of the machine, my immersion in the comforting field of Horse and Wolf energy allowed me to remain calm enough to get through the test without sedation. That was when I knew that I could support other people to learn how to soothe themselves with the power of Wildlife Imagery.

Because I have my Wildlife Imagery and EFT practices to help me manage spikes in my anxiety, I am a much happier person than I once was. And because I am happier inside, I am kinder, more patient, and more open to engaging with others. This is a big win in my marriage and my friendships. I've been happily married for over two decades now, and I can attest to that being a direct result of the time, energy, and commitment I've made to healing myself and creating greater balance.

And now, as an anxiety management therapist, transformational coach, author, and speaker, I have the opportunity to share with others the benefits of the powerful combination of talk therapy, behavioral practices, Wildlife Imagery, and EFT tapping strategies. Way beyond the old playbook of talk therapy and medication alone, the imagery and energy psychology practices can move clients forward faster and make the changes stick.

Opportunities can come in all sizes, shapes, and colors. Sometimes they appear as hardships and other times as gifts. A few of mine have been life-challenging, and a few more lifesaving. Embracing the lesson in each opportunity that presents itself is the key, because there is always a next step in your recovery and evolution.

REFLECTION

What opportunities have you had to go back and try again when things didn't go smoothly? What desired outcomes have you hoped for? When have you been surprised that something amazing worked in your favor? Have you ever asked for guidance? Pleaded with the Universe for an answer to a troubling question? Angled for a convenient parking space? Not every opportunity feels like a gift, but even the challenging ones can lead to improvement. It can feel like a surprise or coincidence when things work out, but maybe you were heard, and it was simply given.

YOUR MEDITATION MANTRA

Whether they may feel like challenges or gifts, all the opportunities I have help me to grow and make me a better person.

ACTION STEPS

When tough situations arise, turn to nature and wildlife for your strength and support. Talk with someone you trust about your struggles, joys, and path toward peace of mind. Rather than remaining in fear and distrust, allow yourself to see, feel, hear, and open to opportunities to develop your flexibility and strength. Sketch drawings of yourself rising above your challenges and enjoying your gifts. These visions in your journal can offer a concrete place for you to reflect on your opportunities. And yes, stick figure drawings will do. You don't need to be a professional artist!

Wedding Day with our "ring bear". Aug 9, 2003

AFTERWORD

Please allow me to bring you up to date with my continued management of anxiety, my continued practice of EFT tapping and other helpful techniques, and the Wildlife Imagery® practice I developed years ago. I frequently call upon my wildlife guides for support and personal power, and I work on my own EFT tapping to keep triggers from becoming mental and physical blocks, which can manifest in all forms of illness and disease. And as I do so, I am circling back again to my childhood friend and wildlife guide, Charlotte, the gray spider in *Charlotte's Web*. When Wilbur the pig asks her why she went to all the trouble of writing fabulous descriptions of him in her web, she explains that by helping Wilbur to be safe from slaughter, she was giving her own life a needed lift, too. Charlotte reminds Wilbur that we can all use a little nudge in the right direction from someone who cares about us.

Happily ever after is a fantasy, and my quest to tame the anxiety beasts has been challenging. But every investment I have made in reclaiming my sanity has been worth it. And I can assure you that I've barely scratched the surface.

Let's look again at that top-shelf crazymaker: cancer.

Staying in the present and continuously working to keep myself calm and grounded allows me to share the following with you. Recently, I had surgery to remove melanoma from my skin for the third time, this time on my left calf. I don't see this as a "three strikes and you're out" event. Instead, I see it as "third time's the charm." Maybe skin cancer is tired of being beaten up and tossed out and will give up for good now.

Always vigilant in making dermatology appointments and following up on anything that looks suspicious, I keep a close eye for any further challenges, and my dermatologist does the same. We both carefully watched the mole on my calf until it showed a slight change in shape. When he said it was time for it to be removed, I was anxious about the surgery and about having to hop around on crutches. I needn't have worried so much about either. The surgery went smoothly, and my friend Cindy loaned me a scooter with a platform to kneel on and support my calf.

After seeing me push myself around on the knee scooter for a few days after the calf surgery, a friend asked, "Do you get scared about melanoma?"

"Hell, no," I replied. "I can't. I don't have time to be scared! I've got too much to do."

And at the middle school where I spend part of my time as an instructional coach, I was a hit with the kids flying around the hallways. The vulnerability of my situation does visit with me, though, for sure. Seeing parts of my body lined with sutures, swollen and bruised, is humbling and could easily set me back. I depend on my stress reduction strategies to help me focus on the present and remember that every excision of my skin is an invitation to stay healthy and be here longer.

I have known since the second and most serious melanoma surgery on the lower left side of my face and neck that the mind-body is fully present under sedation even when we are unconscious. Though we have no active memory of what happens under full sedation, our bodies register and respond to the attack. I have worked through EFT to remove blocks from some of the trauma of that surgery and the pain of the preparation. But I knew there was more to clear, and I did not know how to access it. With the most recent surgery on my calf, I was able to feel the stuck energy from that previous physical and emotional trauma and allow it to move on.

Even though this third outpatient surgery was shorter and smoother, and I planned for it, so I did not have pain with the preparation, my body reacted to being under attack. In the office for the surgery on my calf, I shared goofy stories and listened to some favorite music with my dermatologist, who had been in a band during his college years. And although I walked out without having needed sedation or assistance, happy that it had gone so smoothly, my body began to shake noticeably.

My hands were trembling as I got into my car and gripped the steering wheel. This was my body discharging its tension and fear of being traumatized again after the much more in-depth facial surgery, even though I remember nothing of that ordeal once the sedation took hold. It's fascinating to see how energy in the body and mind is held, coded, and reactivated in us when we don't even realize it's there. And when that energy is negative and fear-based, it lives within us, creating feelings and behaviors that do not serve us.

But there are solutions. Blocked energies can be released through energy psychologies like EFT (Emotional Freedom Techniques) and EMDR (Eye Movement Desensitization and Reprocessing) and touch modalities, including Jin Shin Jyutsu, an ancient Japanese healing art that, like the energy psychologies, clears stress and enhances physical and mental health.

As I move forward from this moment, I'm sure I'm in the right place, at the right time, with all of the history of my eventful life: the difficulties of crazymaking family drama, the manageable health issues that went undiagnosed when I was younger, the overwhelming panic disorder and agoraphobia, and all of the opportunities I continue to have to learn about skin cancer prevention and treatment. Every piece of my history and my present life drives me to help *you* understand the roots of your own struggles, recognize *your* own power to overcome them, and become the balanced person *you* want to be in your world.

My deepest thanks to you for joining me on this journey. I hope that you go back through each chapter, through the reflections, meditation mantras, and action steps to begin your practice and transform your own life. Please share your thoughts and your story with as many people and animals as you can. Create deeper connections every day.

Peace to your heart, My Friend.

RESOURCES

I f you are struggling, please reach out. There is help for all of what you may be feeling.

SUICIDE PREVENTION HOTLINE—DIAL 988

You're not alone. If you don't have someone you feel you can contact about your mental health, that doesn't mean you're alone. Remember that counselors are available 24/7 at the 988 Suicide and Crisis Lifeline. Call 988 or visit *SpeakingOfSuicide.com/resources* for additional resources.

CRISIS TEXT LINE—TEXT AND ONLINE CHAT

The Crisis Text Line is a volunteer-based service that provides 24/7 free support with an online chat at www. crisistextline.org as well as a textable number at 741741.

SAMHSA NATIONAL HELPLINE

SAMHSA (Substance Abuse and Mental Health Services Administration) provides a free twenty-four-hour service in English and Spanish for any mental health or substance abuse related needs. Text: 435748. Call: 1-800-662-4357. TTY: 1-800-487-4889.

NAMI HELPLINE

The NAMI (National Alliance on Mental Illness) provides a volunteer helpline answering questions and offering support for all Mental Illness topics. Call: 800-950-6264. Text: 62640. Email: helpline@nami.org.

PARENTING HOTLINE

Operated by Parents Anonymous. https://www.nationalparenthelpline.org/ Call: 855-427-2736. Email: help@nationalparentyouthhelpline.org.

MENTAL HEALTH HOTLINE

This is a free twenty-four-hour service established to provide resources for those seeking help with anxiety and connection with appropriate, local care. Mental Health Hotline is a hub for several free, reputable anxiety crisis hotline centers available twenty-four hours a day. If you or a loved one is suffering from an anxiety disorder, you deserve to feel better. National Mental Health Hotline: 866-903-3787.

> Please Note: *Connecting with a mental health professional with whom you feel comfortable and safe is key. And, when you're in need of support, it can be tough to see clearly and act accordingly if the relationship is not a good match. Please, don't ever be afraid to end a therapeutic relationship if the connection doesn't feel quite right. A good therapist is as invested in a positive connection with you as you are with yourself.*

ACKNOWLEDGMENTS

Without the editing elegance of Melanie Mulhall (Dragonheart), the publishing prowess of Veronica Yager (Journey Bound Publishing) and the magic touch of Gary Barnes (Gary Barnes International) this book would still be a dream. I appreciate each of you.

My thanks to Tom Petty for providing me with a survival anthem for my life: "I Won't Back Down."

Immense gratitude goes to my childhood neighbor, Carol Gilligan, who was solely responsible for bringing the horses of my imagination to my real life. Your gift changed everything.

I am extremely grateful to Rich Fitzpatrick, PhD, my first therapist, who supported me in identifying and managing my emotions and who set me on the path to easing my anxiety.

My deep appreciation goes to my beta-readers—Dr Jackie Schafer, Tina Brandau, Shameema Patel, Dr Rich Fitzpatrick, Ted Prodromou, Sheral DeVaughn, Gary Barnes, and especially Miriam Zoll—who contributed to this book through the lens of our 50-year friendship.

Special thanks and much love to my husband, Scott. His unwavering kindness and support are constant. He has weathered the storms of my anxiety and never wavered in his belief in me. Thank you for being my definition of faith, hope, and love.

Finally, my thanks to ALL the animals and people who have shown up for me, providing me with love, friendship, and support. And my thanks go out to the animals and people who push my buttons and challenge my belief in myself, who inspire me to be better, to carry on, and to follow my life's true purpose, which is to release myself from the grips of crazymaking anxiety and support others to do the same.

ABOUT BONNIE BRINDLE

THE ANXIETY AVENGER ™

Bonnie Brindle, M. Ed., has been a Colorado psychotherapist with a specialty in equine-assisted therapy and a secondary educator and instructional coach for many years. As her therapy practice has centered mainly on supporting clients struggling with anxiety—with a current focus on dental anxiety—she has followed that path into writing, speaking, and coaching others to release themselves from its grip.

Once trapped in her home and unsure whether life was worth living, Bonnie is a survivor of debilitating anxiety, who can show you how to soar above the crazymaking chaos. A lifelong student of Horse and Wolf and a lover of all things in nature, Bonnie has unlocked the hold of negativity and pain caused by the crazymakers' code—the miserable inheritance that holds many of us back from our full potential. Using the story of her journey through panic disorder, agoraphobia, and a severely limited daily life to arrive at the fullness and joy she lives now, Bonnie is an inspiration and example for those who want to end the suffering caused by crazymakers. She believes every new day is an invitation to live the life you choose.

Bonnie lives in sunny Colorado with her husband Scott and her horse Manchi. Her favorite activities include laughing with friends, staying fit, and savoring dark chocolate. She enjoys her role as her neighborhood critter-sitter and spends as much time in nature and among trees as she can.

Connect with Bonnie:

Bonnie@bonniebrindle.com

www.bonniebrindle.com

HAVE YOU BEEN INSPIRED TO CRACK THE CRAZYMAKERS' CODE?

There are many wonderful therapists and coaches who have written volumes about dealing with anxiety. What makes me different from the rest?

The answer to that is the entirety of why I write, speak, coach and offer a limited number of private therapy sessions. It's why I've created online memberships and courses. My "special sauce" is having negotiated my own life through the lens of debilitating panic disorder and agoraphobia. What informs my understanding is way more than research and education. I have lived the path out of overwhelming anxiety and into a loving marriage and a life filled with friends and opportunities, in which I manage my anxiety daily. Will the challenges ever disappear completely? Will struggle leave you and everything become rosy and easy? Nope.

And I'm not sure if Tom Petty's "gates of hell" are the same as mine, but I won't back down from them, and you don't have to, either. Building your personal resilience and supporting the next generation to crack the crazymakers' code is the recipe for success. This is your time to grow and evolve, to change your story. It's *your* time to soar above the chaos!

Go. Claim it.

LOOKING FOR MORE?

I f you would like to learn about upcoming Soul of
the Wild retreats, our online memberships, home
study courses, or to receive our SPAM-free newslet-
ter, *Musings from the Menagerie*, in your inbox twice a
month, please feel free to join our mailing list at www.
bonniebrindle.com.

Bonnie Brindle is the ideal professional speaker for
your next event. As a psychotherapist, author, national
speaker and transformational coach, her energy, humor,
and commitment to showing your audience how to
crack the crazymakers' code and find peace of mind
is an impactful message. Bonnie uses the power of her
inspirational story to help her audiences begin a path to
reclaim joy and harmony in their lives.

If you'd like to go back through Cracking the
Crazymakers' Code and take the Action Steps for

yourself, you can download your free *Cracking the Crazymakers' Code Journal* at www.BonnieBrindle.com.

FREE GIFT
FROM BONNIE

You are welcome and invited to accept my **Gift of a Free 30-Day Membership in The Anxiety Avenger™ Alliance**. Each month we meet with US and international members for an hour-long Q&A Zoom mastermind call where attendees can ask questions for feedback from me and from the group. Together, we share support and insights, practice strategies, and build our resilience in avenging the crazymaking foundations of anxiety. Our collective goal is to soar above the chaos and reclaim our peace of mind.

Learn more by scanning the QR code below:

Made in United States
North Haven, CT
18 October 2024

59103849R00088